I0813585

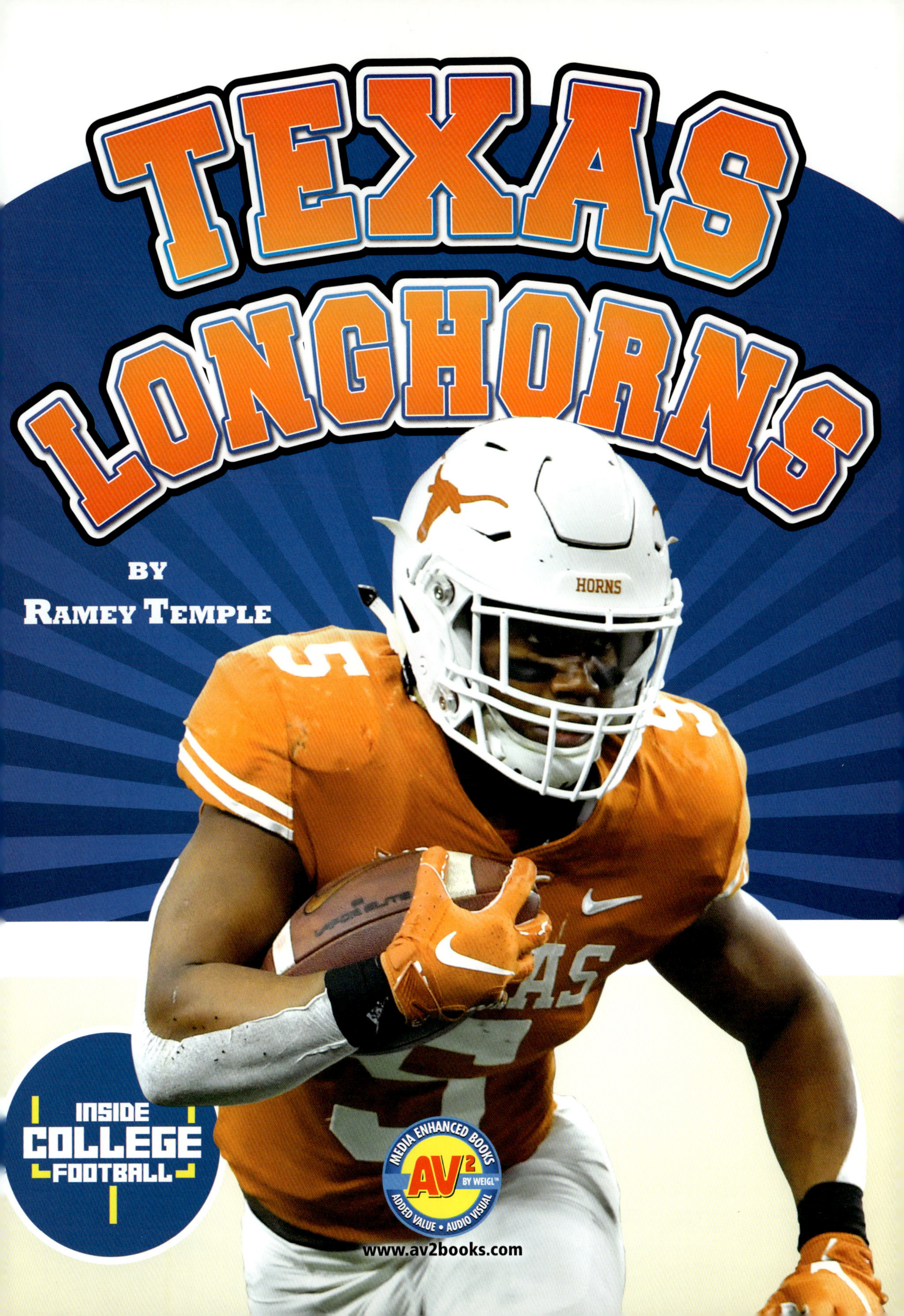
TEXAS
LONGHORNS
BY
RAMEY TEMPLE
HORNS
INSIDE
COLLEGE
FOOTBALL
MEDIA ENHANCED BOOKS
AV2
BY WEIGL
ADDED VALUE • AUDIO VISUAL
www.av2books.com

Go to www.av2books.com, and enter this book's unique code.

BOOK CODE

AVF52492

AV² by Weigl brings you media enhanced books that support active learning.

AV² provides enriched content that supplements and complements this book. Weigl's AV² books strive to create inspired learning and engage young minds in a total learning experience.

Your AV² Media Enhanced books come alive with...

Audio
Listen to sections of the book read aloud.

Video
Watch informative video clips.

Embedded Weblinks
Gain additional information for research.

Try This!
Complete activities and hands-on experiments.

Key Words
Study vocabulary, and complete a matching word activity.

Quizzes
Test your knowledge.

Slideshow
View images and captions, and prepare a presentation.

... and much, much more!

Published by AV² by Weigl
350 5th Avenue, 59th Floor
New York, NY 10118
Website: www.av2books.com

Library of Congress Control Number: 2018968210

ISBN 978-1-7911-0102-2 (hardcover)
ISBN 978-1-7911-0103-9 (multi-user eBook)
ISBN 978-1-7911-0104-6 (single-user eBook)

Printed in Guangzhou, China
1 2 3 4 5 6 7 8 9 0 23 22 21 20 19

042019
102318

Project Coordinator: Jared Siemens   Designer: Terry Paulhus

The publisher acknowledges Alamy, Getty Images, Newscom, and Wikimedia Commons as its primary image suppliers for this title.

Texas Longhorns

CONTENTS

Introduction

The state of Texas is well known as the football capital of America. High school football takes center stage on Friday nights. Saturday, however, is all about the Longhorns. The University of Texas (UT) Longhorns have had a long list of incredible athletes and successful head coaches. Longhorn fans support their team in good times and in bad. However, there have not been many bad seasons. In fact, the Longhorns have the second-most wins in National Collegiate Athletic Association (NCAA) history and have won multiple National Championships.

During the 2015 season, Jerrod Heard became the second player in UT history to throw for 300 yards and rush for 100 yards in a single game.

The Longhorns are a team with many traditions. Displayed at every game is the world's largest Texas flag, measuring 100 feet (30.5 meters) by 150 feet (45.7 m). Big Bertha is the name of the massive bass drum played after each touchdown. Smokey the Cannon fires after every point scored by the Longhorns. These traditions help keep the Texas spirit alive.

Charles Omenihu was named the Big 12 defensive lineman of the year for the 2018 season after logging a career-high 45 tackles.

TEXAS

Stadium Darrell K. Royal–Texas Memorial Stadium

Division Division I Football Bowl Subdivision, Big 12 Conference

Head Coach Tom Herman

Location Austin, Texas

National Championships 3

Nicknames Longhorns, the 'Horns

30 Conference Championships

55 Bowl Games Played

2 Heisman Memorial Trophy Winners

29 Bowl Games Won

History

Coach Darrell K. Royal was named **"Coach of the Decade"** in a 1969 ABC Television poll after winning two National Championships in the 1960s.

Texas plays the University of Oklahoma Sooners every year in a game known as the "Red River Showdown." The longtime rivals compete for the Golden Hat, a trophy featuring a gold cowboy hat. Texas has won the Red River Showdown 62 times.

Steeped in tradition and surrounded by loyal fans, the Longhorns have a rich football history. UT's football program began back in 1893. With a brand-new stadium in 1924 and Head Coach Dana X. Bible's hiring in 1937, the Longhorns were ready to take on the country. The Longhorns became a force under Bible. He led them to bowl-game victories and a handful of Southwest Conference championships.

The 1950s brought Head Coach Darrell K. Royal. This exceptional coach cemented UT's position as a college football powerhouse. The 'Horns won two National Championships between 1963 and 1970. In 1963, they won the National Championship against the United States Naval Academy Midshipmen. In 1969, they won the National Championship again, this time against the University of Notre Dame.

The 1977 season was a great year for UT. It had an undefeated regular season, and Earl Campbell won the university's first Heisman Memorial Trophy. Another big year for the team was 1998. Head Coach Mack Brown was hired, and Ricky Williams won the university's second Heisman. UT won its third National Championship in 2005 and had a run for the title in 2009. Under Coach Tom Herman, 2018 saw a Texas Bowl victory and a winning season for the 'Horns.

During his Heisman Trophy-winning season, Earl Campbell led not only the Longhorns, but also the nation, with 1,744 rushing yards and 19 touchdowns.

The Stadium

The UT band forms a large "T" on the field with space down the middle for players to run through as they enter the field before every home game.

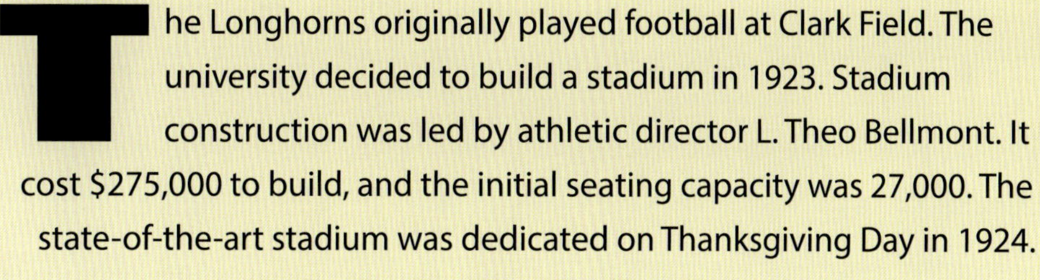

The Longhorns originally played football at Clark Field. The university decided to build a stadium in 1923. Stadium construction was led by athletic director L. Theo Bellmont. It cost $275,000 to build, and the initial seating capacity was 27,000. The state-of-the-art stadium was dedicated on Thanksgiving Day in 1924.

The stadium has gone through many expansions over the years. In 1940, the south-side grandstands were built, increasing the seating capacity to 60,000. Lights were added in 1955, and in 1971, the upper deck was built. In 2009, the south end zone seating was expanded, increasing capacity again. The Moncrief-Neuhaus Athletic Center was also built at the south end of the stadium. This section houses locker rooms, training rooms, a trophy room, and more.

UT students initially named the stadium Memorial Stadium, in honor of all the Texans who fought in **World War I** (1914–1918). In 1977, the stadium was rededicated to veterans of all U.S. wars. The stadium was renamed the Darrell K. Royal–Texas Memorial Stadium in 1966, honoring both the legendary UT coach and continuing to pay tribute to veterans.

Clark Field was originally called Varsity Athletic Field, and multiple sports teams from the University of Texas played there. It served as home of the football team from 1887 until 1924.

Where They Play

Welcome to Darrell K. Royal–Texas Memorial Stadium, home of the Longhorns. It is the biggest stadium in the Big 12 Conference. More than 100,000 fans decked out in orange and white fill the stands for every home game. A record 103,507 people gathered to watch Texas defeat the University of Southern California Trojans in 2018, proof that Longhorns fans love to watch their team dominate in Texas Memorial Stadium.

Arena
Darrell K. Royal–Texas Memorial Stadium

Location
Austin, Texas

Broke Ground
January 1924

Completed
November 8, 1924

Surface
Artificial Turf

Features

- Seating capacity is 100,119
- Video board nicknamed "Godzillatron" above south end zone measures 56 feet (17 meters) high by 135 feet (41 m) wide
- Statues of Heisman winners Ricky Williams and Earl Campbell at southwest corner of stadium

BIG 12

1. **Baylor University** *Waco, Texas*
2. **Iowa State University** *Ames, Iowa*
3. **Kansas State University** *Manhattan, Kansas*
4. **Oklahoma State University** *Stillwater, Oklahoma*
5. **Texas Christian University** *Fort Worth, Texas*
6. **Texas Tech University** *Lubbock, Texas*
7. **University of Kansas** *Lawrence, Kansas*
8. **University of Oklahoma** *Norman, Oklahoma*
9. ☆ **University of Texas at Austin** *Austin, Texas*
10. **West Virginia University** *Morgantown, West Virginia*

VERMONT
NORTH DAKOTA
MONTANA
MINNESOTA
WISCONSIN
MICHIGAN
NEW YORK
SOUTH DAKOTA
WYOMING
PENNSYLVANIA
10
IOWA
OHIO
NEBRASKA
2
ILLINOIS
INDIANA
WEST VIRGINIA
VIRGINIA
3
7
COLORADO
KENTUCKY
KANSAS
MISSOURI
NORTH CAROLINA
TENNESSEE
4
SOUTH CAROLINA
OKLAHOMA
ARKANSAS
NEW MEXICO
MISSISSIPPI
GEORGIA
6
8
ALABAMA
FLORIDA
TEXAS
1
5
LOUISIANA
9
Gulf of Mexico
LEGEND
Home Stadium
Big 12 Team
United States
Other Countries
Water
SCALE
0 miles
500 miles
0 kilometers
500 km

The Uniforms

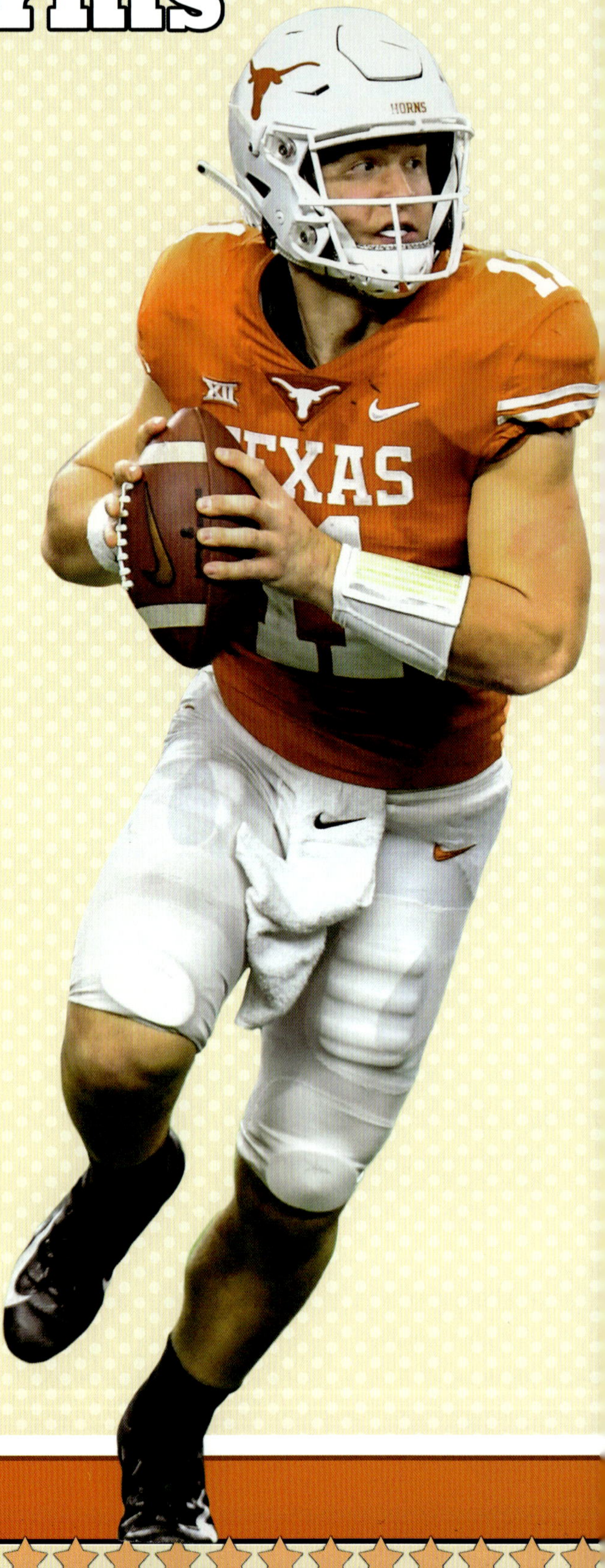

- Texas is one of only a few college football teams with no alternate uniform. It prefers to stick with tradition by sporting only the burnt orange and white colors that have symbolized Texas pride for decades.

Little has changed over the years with the traditional Texas Longhorn uniforms. They have been the same classic orange and white since the team started playing. The university is very particular about its uniforms, including specifying the exact shade of "burnt orange" that is to be used.

Today's uniforms consist of orange jerseys with white stripes on the sleeves and longhorn silhouettes on the front. The players' white pants and white helmets also feature the longhorn silhouette. In 2018, the only small change was to make the word "TEXAS" on the front of the jerseys bigger.

Nike creates the Longhorn uniforms and has done so for many years. In 2015, Nike signed a 15-year licensing and apparel agreement extension for $250 million. Nike supplies all of the apparel and equipment for the entire university.

The longhorn steer logo has been a staple of UT's white helmets since 1961. The longhorn silhouette is one of the most-recognized logos in college sports.

Student Athletes

There are more than **500 student athletes** at the University of Texas.

Defensive lineman Breckyn Hager joined the Longhorns as one of UT's 85 football scholarship recipients in 2015. He is also a philosophy major and an aspiring filmmaker.

Being a student athlete in college is hard work. Student athletes have to perform well on the football field and in the classroom. UT student athletes are required to meet a minimum grade point average and attend all of their classes. Longhorn student athletes have access to Texas Athletics Student Services for tutoring and mentoring. They also have access to the Texas Athletics Nutrition Center, where they can learn how to make good food choices. UT offers many other services to help balance student athletes' lives.

Many student athletes are given athletic scholarships. A scholarship is a financial aid agreement between the athlete and the college or university. Athletes who do not receive an athletic scholarship can be "walk-on" members of the team. This means they are on the team, but without athletic financial aid. UT typically awards the maximum number of football scholarships allowed, which is 85.

Wide receiver Collin Johnson has Longhorns football in his blood. His father, Johnnie Johnson, played football at the University of Texas, and his older brother, Kirk, is one of his teammates.

Bowl Games

Coach Bob Stoops took his team to bowl games in every one of his **18 years** as coach.

Despite entering the 2019 Sugar Bowl as underdogs, the Longhorns defeated the University of Georgia Bulldogs 28–21. It was the second Sugar Bowl victory for UT.

Bowl games are a unique sports tradition in college football. In the beginning of college football, there was no true **postseason**. Today, a variety of postseason bowl games are played. Bowl games give teams the opportunity to continue striving for recognition and victory after the end of regular play. There are currently 40 bowl games played in various combinations each year. These games are chosen with input from teams, sponsors, and the College Football Playoff Selection Committee. The game matchups are announced in December.

The 'Horns played their first bowl game in 1943 at the Cotton Bowl against the Georgia Institute of Technology. UT has had its most bowl appearances in the Cotton Bowl, and its most common opponent has been the University of Alabama Crimson Tide. The Longhorns are number one in the Big 12 for bowl appearances, with a bowl record of 29–24–2.

Texas fell to longtime rivals the Alabama Crimson Tide in the 2010 Bowl Championship Series (BCS) National Championship Game.

The Coaches

The Longhorns have had **30 head coaches** over the years.

In just two seasons, Tom Herman transformed the Longhorns into a winning team, leading them to two bowl wins, a top-10 ranking, and a spot in the Big 12 championship game.

The Longhorns have been coached by strong leaders who each left a permanent mark on the football program. Dana X. Bible coached the team for 10 seasons and helped bring the team to national prominence. Legendary coach Darrell K. Royal did not have a single losing season during his 23 years as coach. Coach Mack Brown had 158 career victories over 16 seasons. Current head coach Tom Herman has led the Longhorns since 2017.

DANA X. BIBLE Dana X. Bible was the UT coach from 1937 to 1946. During this time, the Longhorns made three Cotton Bowl appearances and won three Southwest Conference championships. Bible was also the president of the American Football Coaches Association and was inducted into the College Football **Hall of Fame** in 1951. His overall record was 63–31–3.

DARRELL K. ROYAL Darrell K. Royal is the most famous Longhorn coach. Royal was hired as head coach in 1956. The team went on to win 11 Southwest Conferences, 10 Cotton Bowls, and two National Championships during his reign. Royal had a 167–47–5 record during his time at UT. He retired in 1976 and was inducted into the College Football Hall of Fame in 1983.

MACK BROWN Mack Brown was head coach from 1998 to 2013. He had one of UT's most successful coaching records. Under Brown, the Longhorns won two Big 12 championships. They also won the 2005 National Championship and played in the 2009 National Championship game. Brown won many awards, including the 2009 Big 12 Coach of the Year. He was inducted into the College Football Hall of Fame in 2018.

The Mascot

Bevo XV is does not mind the huge crowds at Longhorns games and other UT events. He even attends graduation ceremonies.

UT's mascot is Bevo XV, a live longhorn steer. Bevo XV made his debut in 2016 and is the 15th live Longhorns mascot in more than 100 years. The first Bevo debuted in 1916. Every Bevo has had burnt orange and white coloring, representing the school colors. Bevo even attends pep rallies and other university events. Since 1946, each Bevo has been brought to football games by a group of handlers called the Silver Spurs. The school's battle cry, "Hook 'em Horns," was inspired by the steer mascot. There is also a Hook 'em Horns hand signal used by fans that **mimics** the shape of Bevo's head and horns.

The Longhorns have a second mascot, a costumed longhorn steer named Hook 'Em. He debuted in the 1970s and is known for his dance moves. He even starred in a music video with country singer Brad Paisley.

The student who portrays Hook 'Em must be in excellent physical shape. Hook 'Em not only dances and does cartwheels on the field during games, but also leads the team onto the field before kickoff and interacts with fans before, during, and after games.

Legends of the Past

For many players, their time with the Longhorns is the start of a promising football career. These are some of the best-known football players to play for the University of Texas.

Ricky Williams

Two-time **All-American** running back Ricky Williams set 21 NCAA records during his time as a Longhorn. He won NCAA rushing titles in both 1997 and 1998. He is one of only two UT Heisman Trophy winners. Williams was **drafted** by the New Orleans Saints in 1999 and spent 11 seasons in the National Football League (NFL). He holds the Miami Dolphins' single-season franchise records for rushing yards and rushing touchdowns. He retired after the 2011 season with 10,009 rushing yards and 74 touchdowns. In 2015, he was inducted into the College Football Hall of Fame.

Position: Running Back
Seasons: 1995–1998 (UT Longhorns), 1999–2001 (New Orleans Saints), 2002–2005 (Miami Dolphins), 2006 (Canadian Football League Toronto Argonauts), 2007–2010 (Miami Dolphins), 2011 (Baltimore Ravens)
Born: May 21, 1977, San Diego, California

Earl Campbell

Earl Campbell was one of UT's most popular players. A consensus All-American, he won the Heisman Trophy in 1977. During his sophomore year, Campbell helped UT secure its 10–2 record. He was the best in the nation in both scoring and rushing during his senior year. Campbell was drafted by the Houston Oilers in 1978. After his impressive first season, he was named NFL **Most Valuable Player (MVP)**, **All-Pro**, and Rookie of the Year. He went on to play for the New Orleans Saints, and retired from the NFL in 1985.

Position: Running Back
Seasons: 1974–1977 (UT Longhorns), 1978–1984 (Houston Oilers), 1984–1985 (New Orleans Saints)
Born: March 29, 1955, Tyler, Texas

Earl Thomas

While in college at UT, safety Earl Thomas was a Freshman All-American. As a sophomore, he helped the Longhorns win the Big 12 Conference title. That year, the team was 13–1 and came up just short of the national title against the Alabama Crimson Tide. After his sophomore season, Thomas was drafted by the Seattle Seahawks in the first round of the 2010 NFL draft. Thomas has been to the **Super Bowl** twice, helping the Seahawks win their first-ever Super Bowl in 2013 against the Denver Broncos. In 2017, he was named to his sixth **Pro Bowl**.

Position: Safety
Seasons: 2007–2009 (UT Longhorns), 2010–Present (Seattle Seahawks)
Born: May 7, 1989, Orange, Texas

Marquise Goodwin

Marquise Goodwin is an all-around athlete. Not only is he a great football player, but he was also a major track and field star. He played both sports at UT. Goodwin was part of the UT football team that went to the 2009 National Championship under coach Brown. While at UT, he also won the long jump at the 2012 U.S. Olympic Trials and finished 10th in the London Olympics. Goodwin then decided to go pro in football, and was a third-round draft pick by the Buffalo Bills in 2013. He signed a four-year contract with the Bills, and then a three-year contract with the San Francisco 49ers in 2017.

Position: Wide Receiver
Seasons: 2009–2012 (UT Longhorns), 2013–2016 (Buffalo Bills), 2017–Present (San Francisco 49ers)
Born: November 19, 1990, Lubbock, Texas

All-Time Records

6,279

Career Rushing Yards

School running back legend Ricky Williams had 6,279 rushing yards by the time he left UT.

8

Single-Season Interceptions

During his last year at UT, Earl Thomas had eight single-season interceptions.

4

Single-Game Receiving Touchdowns

One of UT's best wide receivers, Wane McGarity has many entries in the Texas record books, including four single-game receiving touchdowns.

15

Single-Game Receptions

Jordan Shipley, an All-American wide receiver, broke the UT record with 15 receptions in a 2008 game against the Oklahoma State University Cowboys.

499

Career Tackles

Britt Hager is the Longhorns all-time leading tackler, with 499 career tackles. Hager also holds the record for most tackles in a single season.

Timeline

Throughout the team's history, the Texas Longhorns have had many memorable events that have become defining moments for the team and its fans.

1963
UT wins the National Championship for the first time against the Navy Midshipmen.

1893
UT's football program begins with its first game against the Dallas Foot Ball Club.

1937
Dana X. Bible, a well-known and established college football coach, is hired as head coach.

1900 1920 1940 1960

Bevo, the first live mascot, debuts during a game versus the Texas A&M Aggies in 1916.

1924
Memorial Stadium is built to allow for more seating and to create a more permanent home for the Longhorns.

1969
The Longhorns win the National Championship against the Notre Dame Fighting Irish.

2005
The 'Horns win the National Championship against the University of Michigan Wolverines in the Rose Bowl.

The Future
Head Coach Herman was hired in 2016 and signed a five-year contract with the Longhorns. In 2017, the Longhorns had their first winning season since 2013, with a record of 7–6. They finished the 2018 season ranked ninth in the nation, with a win in the Sugar Bowl over the University of Georgia Bulldogs. The Longhorns are gaining momentum and are looking to get back onto the national stage.

1980 2000 2020

1977
Earl Campbell wins UT's first Heisman Trophy after helping his team have an undefeated regular season.

In 1998, Ricky Williams leads the nation in rushing and wins UT's second Heisman Trophy.

2017
UT wins the Texas Bowl against the University of Missouri Tigers.

2009
The Longhorns win the Big 12 Conference and play in the Bowl Championship Series National Championship Game.

Write a Biography

Life Story

A person's life story can be the subject of a book. This kind of book is called a biography. Biographies often describe the lives of people who have achieved great success. These people may be alive today, or they may have lived many years ago. Reading a biography can help you learn more about a great person.

Get the Facts

Use this book, and research in the library and on the internet, to find out more about your favorite player. Learn as much about him as you can. What position does he play? What are his statistics in important categories? Has he set any records? Also, be sure to write down key events in the person's life. What was his childhood like? What has he accomplished off the field? Is there anything else that makes this person special or unusual?

Use the Concept Web

A concept web is a useful research tool. Read the questions in the concept web on the following page. Answer the questions in your notebook. Your answers will help you write a biography.

Concept Web

Adulthood
- Where does this individual currently reside?
- Does he have a family?

Your Opinion
- What did you learn from the books you read in your research?
- Would you suggest these books to others?
- Was anything missing from these books?

Childhood
- Where and when was this person born?
- Describe his parents, siblings, and friends.
- Did he grow up in unusual circumstances?

Accomplishments off the Field
- What is this person's life's work?
- Has he received awards or recognition for accomplishments?
- How have this person's accomplishments served others?

Write a Biography

Help and Obstacles
- Did this individual have a positive attitude?
- Did he receive help from others?
- Did this person have a mentor?
- Did this person face any hardships?
- If so, how were the hardships overcome?

Accomplishments on the Field
- What records does he hold?
- What key games and plays have defined his career?
- What are his stats in categories important to his position?

Work and Preparation
- What was this person's education?
- What was his work experience?
- How does this person work?
- What is the process he uses?

Trivia Time

Take this quiz to test your knowledge of the Texas Longhorns. The answers are printed upside down under each question.

1 When is Big Bertha played at football games?

A. After every touchdown

2 What is the full name of the Longhorns' stadium?

A. Darrell K. Royal–Texas Memorial Stadium

3 What is the nickname for the large video board at the stadium?

A. "Godzillatron"

4 Who creates the Longhorns' uniforms?

A. Nike

5 How many seasons did Dana X. Bible coach the 'Horns?

A. 10

6 What is the name of the group that brings Bevo to every football game?

A. The Silver Spurs

7 Which UT football legend was also a track and field star?

A. Marquise Goodwin

8 What is the name of the cannon that fires after every Longhorn score?

A. Smokey the Cannon

9 What country music star featured Hook 'Em in one of his music videos?

A. Brad Paisley

10 When did the UT football program begin?

A. 1893

Key Words

All-American: a player, usually in high school or college, judged to be the best in each position of a sport

All-Pro: a term used to designate the best players of each position during a given season

drafted: chosen to play professionally in the National Football League during an annual event

Hall of Fame: a group of persons judged to be outstanding in a particular sport

mimics: to imitate someone's actions or words

Most Valuable Player (MVP): the player judged to be most valuable to his team's success

postseason: a sporting event that takes place after the end of the regular season

Pro Bowl: the annual all-star game for NFL players pitting the best players in the National Football Conference against the best players in the American Football Conference

Super Bowl: the NFL's annual championship game between the winning team from the National Football Conference and the winning team from the American Football Conference

World War I: a war fought in Europe and the Middle East between the Allies (France, Russia, Great Britain, Italy, Japan, and the United States) and the Central Powers (Germany, Austria-Hungary, and Turkey)

Index

Log on to www.av2books.com

AV² by Weigl brings you media enhanced books that support active learning. Go to www.av2books.com, and enter the special code found on page 2 of this book. You will gain access to enriched and enhanced content that supplements and complements this book. Content includes video, audio, weblinks, quizzes, a slideshow, and activities.

AV² Online Navigation

Audio
Listen to sections of the book read aloud.

Book Pages
AV² pages directly correspond to pages in the book.

Video
Watch informative video clips.

Embedded Weblinks
Gain additional information for research.

Key Words
Study vocabulary, and complete a matching word activity.

Try This!
Complete activities and hands-on experiments.

Quizzes
Test your knowledge.

Slideshow
View images and captions, and prepare a presentation.

AV² was built to bridge the gap between print and digital. We encourage you to tell us what you like and what you want to see in the future.

Sign up to be an AV² Ambassador at www.av2books.com/ambassador.

Due to the dynamic nature of the internet, some of the URLs and activities provided as part of AV² by Weigl may have changed or ceased to exist. AV² by Weigl accepts no responsibility for any such changes. All media enhanced books are regularly monitored to update addresses and sites in a timely manner. Contact AV² by Weigl at 1-866-649-3445 or av2books@weigl.com with any questions, comments, or feedback.